AF077265

SPIRITUAL OARS
for
DARK WATERS

Christians Successfully Navigating
the Corporate World of Work

Pastor Keith D. Wright Sr. PhD.

Copyright © 2016 by Pastor Keith D. Wright Sr. PhD.

Spiritual Oars for Dark Waters
Christians Successfully Navigating the Corporate World of Work
by Pastor Keith D. Wright Sr. PhD.

Printed in the United States of America.

ISBN 9781498482523

All rights reserved solely by the author. The author guarantees all contents are original and do not infringe upon the legal rights of any other person or work. No part of this book may be reproduced in any form without the permission of the author. The views expressed in this book are not necessarily those of the publisher.

Unless otherwise indicated, Scripture quotations taken from the King James Version (KJV)–*public domain.*

Scripture quotations taken from the Holy Bible, New Living Translation (NLT). Copyright ©1996, 2004, 2007 by Tyndale House Foundation. Used by permission of Tyndale House Publishers, Inc.

www.xulonpress.com

Contents

Foreword vii
Dedication xi
Introduction xiii
Character 23
Choosing your Company 37
Clarify the Rules 43
Calling All Mentors 49
Creating Your Brand 57
Creating and Adding Value 63
Celebrate the Giver by sharing your Gifts 70
Culture and Organizational Change 76
Connecting the Dots 82
Community is Still Possible 90
Bibliography 103

Foreword

This book is written during a moment of great national anxiety and despair. The uncertainty of the nation's future is certainly impacting the American worker as a global economy breeds anxiety. As corporations increase their footprint in our society and exact a toll on the quality of life of citizens in the form of the abuse of the natural environment, exploitation of foreign workers, income inequality and betraying the hard earned pensions of retirees – there is a yearning among the masses for meaning in the morass.

Every day the American worker who walks into an office suite is challenged by the need to earn a living, and the desire for recognition of her or his labor, and the need to embrace all the external elements of life that define what makes our experience on this earth human. It is a conflict not easily resolved and one that perplexes individuals who work in the private sector. For persons of faith that dilemma cuts even deeper and forces a greater degree of introspection.

This book, written from the perspective of a Christian minister and disciple, really probes the question: "How do I use my holy gifts and preserve my spirituality in the workplace?" Though based upon the foundation of Christianity, this book is relevant for people of all faiths. For those who believe in a higher power, a greater good, walk a tightrope when encountering the profit-driven motivations of America's corporate sector. How does one reconcile their faith when the focus of their work lives contradicts much of what is expected of them in the exercise of that faith? Do we betray our principles for the sake of material gain – higher salary, corner office, executive title and perks? Must we sacrifice our souls for the good of the company?

Yes, many of us are wading in the dark waters of corporate America and the only way we can navigate the treacherous currents of capitalism is to lean on our spiritual oars to help us arrive safely to shore.

Rev. Keith Wright explores the inner conflicts of a Christian in the workforce, and uses the Scriptures to give us a roadmap on how to reconcile the daily pressures of the office with our faith. It is no easy task, but Wright lays out in clear thought and faith a template that can be used to guide us and bring us to a point of understanding that our faith is an asset in the workplace. We do not have to leave our faith in the corporate lobby but instead embed it in how we approach our employment, develop our daily work habits, manage our expectations and define our success. In this book Rev. Wright brings clarity to what is means to be a Disciple in the office and how our faith is the source of our strength in the corporate setting.

"And they will know we are Christians by our love" is the chorus of a song that seeks to connect us as Christians in a world corrupted by evil. When we walk into an office we forget that the greatest representation of our faith is not in our witness, but in our actions. Do we engage honestly and respectfully with our co-workers? Are we good counsel to those who have difficulty navigating office politics? Do we find constructive ways to object to practices of our employer when they harm people? Are we mute when we see our colleagues treated unfairly, denied promotions or discriminated against because of their race, gender or sexual orientation? Do we provide our employer with an honest day's work in exchange for our wages and benefits?

These are much harder questions to consider and a more difficult positioning of our faith than having a Bible on our desk and asking a colleague "Do you know Jesus?" When we take the lessons of Sunday morning worship and truly integrate our faith in the daily practice of our professional lives through the week, we can shift the atmosphere of corporate America and uplift humankind. If we can get beyond the inner conflict we often feel in the office and tap our faith to show spiritual leadership that does not have to conflict with our roles and responsibilities, our employers and those that purchase its services will benefit. Instead of thinking of our Christianity as something we must put on display in the office, we fulfill the word by seamlessly integrating the teachings of Jesus Christ into our workplace relationships, the tasks we are given, and our performance as an employee. It is the example we set of walking in faith that allows the skeptic, the non-believer and the wavering to find hope in the message of Christ.

This book is written in the best tradition of Christian witness. I can attest that Rev. Wright is giving us a prophetic vision for corporate practices because I have witnessed his walk. He has practiced what he is preaching. He has been penalized for it and has remained faithful throughout his personal trials. I know him to be a living witness for Christ because he provided me with some spiritual oars when the dark waters of corporate life engulfed me. In a day and age when we rely on technology for guidance, Rev. Wright reminds us that our most reliable GPS is the Scriptures. I commend this book for those who feel lost in their professional lives, who feel in conflict with their faith in the workplace, and who simply want to do what is pleasing in the sight of God at all times.

Walter Fields
Maplewood, New Jersey
August 2016

Dedication

This book is dedicated to my sister
Karen (Deeta) Denise Chandler
who passed away on January 8, 2006.
In April 1986 on the occasion of a significant promotion she gave
me a miniature typewriter and a note that read

Dear Keith,
It's great you've got
A brand new job
Let's hope it
Brings you joy!
Remember work, work, work
And little or no play
Will make Keith a
Very dull boy!

So here's a
Little something
To give your play some luster
A really portable typewriter

And your personal
Typewriter duster!

Congratulations!!!
Love,
Karen

At the bottom of the card she wrote,
"Take time to pursue your writing."
Thank you, Sis, for your inspiration, support,
and encouragement—I love you still.

Whatever you do, work at it with all your heart, as working for the Lord, not for men, since you know that you will receive an inheritance from the Lord as a reward. It is the Lord Christ you are serving. Colossians 3:23–24 (NLT)

Introduction

Why write a book on navigating corporate America in a self-proclaimed Christian nation that uses the Bill of Rights first amendment language of separation between church and state purely for political purposes? I am glad you asked, and I am particularly glad you are holding this book in search of the answer. This book is directed towards Christians and people of faith.

Today it has become increasingly clear that the American corporation will impact much more than our individual lives. While many will spend a third or more of each day earning a living, they must understand the trade-offs that can occur between their career and their calling.

The desire to live and pursue a life of passion, integrity, loyalty, honesty, security, and abundance, while honorable and worthy goals, can easily be replaced with greed, deceit, selfishness, mistrust, and betrayal inside the corporate workplace.

Hollywood's attraction to storylines with titles such as *Scandal*, *Lie to Me*, *House of Cards*, *Empire,* and *How to Get Away with Murder* to name a few, while offered as purely entertainment, do not require much imagination or rewriting to distinguish Hollywood stories from the dark reality and history of the corporate world.

The political fights between trade agreements versus job protection and continued prosperity for America's middle class have their origins in the collective decisions and choices made by corporate and political leaders. The history of corporate America is an ugly history of greed, graft, corruption, political favoritism, deceit, and destruction.

While society has attempted to filter out the corruption, and clean the environment of the corporate world, over the years, the waters are still murky, muddy, and dark in too many companies. The person of faith has to determine how best to navigate the myriad of choices presented in the work environment and how to successfully navigate towards those that align with one's faith.

Job seekers, especially those beginning their careers, should have a basic understanding of the motivation that drives and determines the executive choices of the leadership with respect to the direction and growth of the business or industry of their interest.

While some historians applaud the first politicians for their desire to keep a separation between church and state, today's historians will have to admit that the corporate domination and control of America's culture is just as pervasive, if not more so, than the threat of religious control.

When the question is asked, what drives the American culture? One may hear romantic terms like individualism, ruggedness, self-starter, Horatio Alger, and rags-to-riches stories. It is unlikely that you will hear that our culture is driven by corporate greed and the love of money, yet billions are spent on commercials and advertising in an effort to create, convince or control public opinion.

It is even less likely that you will hear that our largest institutions, our government, our political parties, our churches, and our media

Introduction

are all corporate-run institutions whose first priority is to keep the corporation alive.

There is a myth that history repeats itself; in reality, people repeat the mistakes of history. It is a Romanticized view of American culture to say that we are "one united nation indivisible under God."

Organized (corporate) religion in America is represented by millions of Christians who, after they conclude their weekly Sunday or Saturday service, disappear into the fabric of their community or corporation only to reappear in time to, once again, corporately practice their doctrine during Easter and Christmas.

There are many professed Christians who are members of Congress, which is arguably America's most powerful corporation, yet the output of their collective efforts to consistently support a war economy over a community restorative economy speaks of their loyalty to the corporation.

An elected congress of 535 men and women sit (some for decades) and control and direct the spending of our tax dollars. Year after year, billions of federal dollars are directed toward the interest of the controlling party. Notice, I did not say the party in control.

"What drives American culture?" is the question posed at the beginning of this discussion. I submit to you that corporations are the unseen hand at the helm, steering our culture in a way that sustains corporations at all cost. Dr. King argued that economic exploitation, militarism, and racism were three evils that continued to pervade the American culture.

Our society continues to debate the economic impacts of partial unemployment versus full-employment security for all who desire to work.

Whether or not the debate reaches your home remains uncertain. One thing, however, is certain, and that is the choice of where you decide to work should satisfy more than a monetary need.

The corporate world, despite its history and challenges, can be navigated successfully with the proper tools and teammates.

Our current environment of extensive labor laws, required postings of equal employment opportunity, diversity and inclusion, and a discrimination-free workplace seem to suggest that once I am hired and onboard, the hard work is over.

If I show up to work on time and follow the guidance of my supervisors, I am destined to succeed. I have a good starting salary, great benefits, and a human resources department ready, able, and willing to provide real-time career assistance each step of my journey.

Hey, you need to hit the alarm button; wake up and swallow the coffee.

Corporate dreams come true when they are accompanied by a results-oriented action plan that is designed with prayer and purpose that makes room for your goals and your gifts and that aligns with the best intentions of the corporate world and your calling.

Doesn't sound like the place you call work? Don't despair, you are not alone—I'm not kidding, you are not alone.

Now that I have your attention, the first bit of information that you need to lock into your memory bank as it relates to working in a corporate environment is, it's not about you.

Yes, I understand that you have an impressive résumé and an awesome rolodex with a wireless Bluetooth connection to your PDA, tablet, or smartphone. You have worked all the angles. You have completed the orientation requirements for new hires and now you

Introduction

are ready to flash your ID badge (business cards will be available in a week) to the waiting world.

Congratulations, well done, you have come to the end of you and the beginning of the corporate icon. Check your ID badge, it will state that you are icon number 247301, 17283, or 04284.

"Remember, it is not about you."

I understand very well your wish to dispute and claim that you have worked in such and such corporation for several years and that you have held key positions.

You may also argue that it was a combination of your talents and skills that positively impacted the direction of the corporation and as a result your imprint is all over the corporation.

During your retirement party (if you are fortunate to have one) your family and friends will listen as the CEO (the fourth during your tenure) speaks glowing accolades about your contributions.

Congratulations and well done. Prayerfully, your patience and determination to succeed were adequately rewarded by the corporation.

Your corporate icon number 999, 1001, or 10200 has now moved to the inactive file. You are special, and there is no doubt that you did some great work. However, at the end of the corporate day it is not about you.

If you have heard the comment, it's not personal it's just business, more than likely, the comment originated from a business decision that went against the best interest of the employee.

I know that it is a hard pill to swallow for some individuals, particularly people of faith, however, my hope is that if you understand this reality early in your career then you can save valuable time, minimize frustration, and perhaps make the corporation(s) work for you, as they will certainly make you work for them. Stay with me and I will explain.

Corporations are created as self-sustaining entities. Webster defines them as, "a body formed and authorized by law to act as a single person although constituted by one or more persons and legally endowed with various rights and duties including the capacity of succession." (Webster, 1991)

Regardless of who comes through the door or exits the door, the corporation is wired to create and recreate itself.

Even though the mutable power of the traditional corporation appears indestructible and can wreck untold havoc on nations, individuals, families, and communities, it is my prayer and firm belief that, like a category five hurricane weakens and returns to the sea, unchecked global corporate power, as we know it, will ultimately be weakened and removed from our collective communities.

My optimism is grounded both in my faith and in the reality that more and more people will look behind the corporate curtain and find as Dorothy did in the "Wizard of Oz" story that there was a man pulling all of the levers that frustrated, stalled, and otherwise impacted her destiny and her journey home.

Dorothy, like most of us in the corporate world, was led to believe that the entity known as the Wizard had complete power to guide her, and her companions, to a safe and comfortable environment called home.

The individual attempting to navigate the corporate structure in search of a fulfilling job or, better still, a rewarding career, must first understand the role of the traditional corporation.

Introduction

It exists to be served not to serve. The corporation, unlike the Kingdom of Christ, seeks to be served. Christians understand that Christ want us to live a life of serving.

"For even the Son of Man came not to be served but to serve others and to give his life as a ransom for many" (Mark 10:45, NLT).

You may be thinking, what, then, is the problem–the corporation wants to be served, and the Christian wants to serve—a perfect match.

Not quite; the corporation's narrow focus on greed and growth are directly opposed to the goodness, grace, and glory of God's kingdom. You, as a believer, must always remember that you are serving for the greater good and to usher in the glory of Christ.

> *"Whatever you do, work at it with all your heart, as working for the Lord, not for men, since you know that you will receive an inheritance from the Lord as a reward. It is the Lord Christ you are serving" (Colossians 3:23–24, NLT).*

I use the qualifier *traditional* corporation as a way to acknowledge there has been, for several decades, a movement towards greater integrity, people-oriented, servant-led, and a principal-centered and balanced organizational framework.

Authors and leaders such as Benjamin Elijah Mays, Robert K. Greenleaf, Steven Covey, Maya Angelou, C. Gene Wilks, Todd G. Gongwer, George Barna, John Maxwell, and so many others are credited for sustaining the momentum in such a positive direction.

Perhaps they understood the words of Christ in Matthew 23:11 that say, **"But he that is greatest among you shall be your servant" (KJV).**

While the benefits of a successful corporate career can yield enormous financial, political, and social gains, the flip side is also true. A successful corporate career can produce enormous stress, dissatisfaction, and disillusionment.

Christ's admonitions, **"For what shall it profit a man, if he shall gain the whole world, and lose his own soul? Or what shall a man give in exchange for his soul?" (Mark 8:36–37, KJV)** should be uppermost in our thoughts and minds as we seek to navigate our way through the channels and challenges of the corporate world.

At each step of the way it is the sole responsibility of the individual to make the final call regarding one's place of employment and to own the decisions that will impact one's career.

To decide is to kill off all other options and move forward. The choice is yours to make!

Utilizing your God given talents to help others, while also being blessed, is a wonderful thing. Conversely, compromising your gifts or selling them to the highest bidder to acquire material possessions, while it may be common in our culture, it is not Christ-like.

> **"For what shall it profit a man, if he shall gain the whole world, and lose his own soul?" (Mark 8:36, KJV).**

It is my desire to share with you some of the lessons and insights gained from my experiences, with several major corporations, over

Introduction

the past three decades with the hope that I can help you remain focused on what truly matters.

The history of the corporate world, despite its best efforts outlined in their social responsibility documents or expensively produced annual reports, is a history fraught with greed, scandal, deceit, and in some cases death and destruction.

This history is glossed over as millions of individuals are unemployed and each year a continuous wave of college graduates and new immigrants seek to enter the labor market.

Seeking and selecting a place to offer one's talents and skills is an important decision that impacts both the individual and their family. The ability to choose wisely is my prayer for you as you navigate the murky waters of the corporate world.

I offer you these spiritual oars to guide your journey as you define and shape the destiny of your career and contributions.

Character is our first spiritual oar.

Character

"Character plus intelligence is the true goal of education" (Dr. Martin Luther King Jr.)

While the dictionary may describe *character* as, *"the aggregate of features and traits that form the individual nature of a person or thing . . . while it may point to special features or traits; While it may even address moral or ethical qualities,"* we are defining it according to a quote I read years ago, "Character is what you do when you think no one is looking."

As an eighth grade student, I was surrounded by various quotations that our homeroom teacher had placed around the perimeter of the classroom.

Directly in front of my desk, each morning, I looked at the quote, **"Character is what you do when you think no one is looking."**

My insight of the quote, as an eighth grader, was simply, "don't get caught when you are playing practical jokes on your classmates."

Thankfully, I have matured over the years to learn that the quote was providing insight into one of life's critical lessons: character matters.

Whether we openly acknowledge or quietly ignore our observations of each other, the subject of character is always present in our mind. Therefore, it is important to know that the character of an individual or of a corporation matters.

When we have conversations about entities or co-workers we often speak in terms of their behavior, their personalities, their gifts, their accomplishments, and their profits or possessions, however, when we get up close and personal, as in joining an organization or marrying into a certain family, the conversation for most of us switches directly to character.

Character Matters.

Your Character is the one thing that always remains under your control. You and only you are the architect of your character.

When I think of character I am reminded of Hebrews 13:8, **"Jesus Christ is the same yesterday, today, and forever." (NLT)**

The writer of Hebrews is telling us that there is a trustworthy consistency in the behavior and character of Jesus.

He lets us know that we can check his past behavior, we can examine his present behavior, or we expect his future behavior to all be consistently aligned.

Jesus provided for all who would examine his ways and his words a genuine consistency and authenticity. When we read the accounts of his life in the bible we find that people were drawn to him expecting and believing he would bring healing and comfort to the things causing them misery and pain.

Wherever Jesus traveled crowds would gather in anticipation of what they expected him to do. Jesus would not fail them, rather he would maintain a character of consistency from place to place.

Character

> **Early the next morning Jesus went out to an isolated place. The crowds searched everywhere for him, and when they finally found him, they begged him not to leave them.**
>
> **But he replied, "I must preach the Good News of the Kingdom of God in other towns, too, because that is why I was sent."**
>
> **So he continued to travel around, preaching in synagogues throughout Judea. Luke 4:42–44 (NLT)**

As Christians who happen to be corporate workers we must give serious thought to the consistency of our character. In a sermon series on character a pastor asked the following questions:

I. What are the distinguishing marks of a Christian?
A. How can we tell when someone is a Christian and when someone is not?
B. More importantly, how can we tell if we are aligned to the Word of God?

Christ Gave Us Our Answer:

> **You can identify them by their fruit, that is, by the way they act. Can you pick grapes from thornbushes, or figs from thistles? A good tree produces good fruit, and a bad tree produces bad fruit. A good tree can't produce bad fruit, and a bad tree can't produce good fruit. (Matthew 7:16–18, NLT)**

Some of you may be asking at this point, is the author asking us to bring our religious practices and traditions into the workplace?

Is he asking us to evangelize and convert others while we work. The answer is a resounding no!

What the author is stressing, is that you should remain true (genuine) to who you are and what you believe (authentic) despite the environment you find yourself placed in.

Our character is to be shaped from the inside out not from the outside in. We must be extremely careful and discerning not to let the character of the organization displace or consume our character when the organizations' character is toxic.

You may be thinking, how can one see the character of a corporation. Glad you asked that question.

We must always remember that despite the fact the corporation is shielded within a legal framework, it is run and managed by individuals just like you and me.

The character of the corporation is manifested in, and through, the corporate culture (We will talk more about culture later).

Many corporations and individuals may start out with great character, but then an adversary or a competitor draws them away from their consistency.

We know we have an adversary named Satan who wants us to walk contrary to our Godly calling, but we must remember and acknowledge Satan is:

- Deceptive
- Disingenuous
- Distrustful
- Disruptive
- Disrespectful

- Devious
- Dishonest
- And most importantly, Satan is a distraction.

He has a singular goal and that is to take you and me to hell with him! We need to hear the words of James when he says, "Submit yourselves therefore to God. Resist the devil, and he will flee from you" (James 4:7, KJV).

Our ability to remain true to ourselves while working inside the corporate world is challenged by the dark history and the underlying character and culture of the corporation.

Biblical scholar Obery Hendricks Jr. in his book, *The Politics of Jesus*, points out how poor character on the part of capitalist led to deplorable working conditions for the masses of American workers:

> **These capitalist became so rapacious and the plight of working American so deplorable that on July 4, 1876, the Workingmen's Party of Illinois issued a Centennial Declaration of Independence. It declared in part:**
>
> **The present system has enabled capitalists to make laws in their own interests to the injury and oppression of the workers.**
>
> **It has made the name of Democracy, for which our forefathers fought and died, a mockery and a shadow, by giving to [those with wealth and]**

property a disproportionate amount of representation and control over Legislation.

It has allowed the capitalists, as a class, to appropriate annually 5/6 of the entire production of the country.

It has, therefore, prevented mankind from fulfilling their natural destinies on earth—crushed out ambition, prevented marriages or caused false and unnatural ones—has shortened human life, destroyed morals and fostered crime, corrupted judges, ministers, and statesmen, shattered confidence, love and honor among men, and made life a selfish, merciless struggle for existence instead of a noble and generous struggle for perfection, in which equal advantages should be given to all, and human lives relieved from an unnatural and degrading competition for bread. (Hendricks, 2006)

When we compare the inconsistent treatment of the capitalist towards the worker, in the previous quote, with the consistent treatment of Jesus towards the crowds that pursued him, we find a major gap in the treatment of our fellow human beings.

The underlying cause for the disparity can be traced back to the character and the motivations of the individuals involved.

The capitalists are motivated by control, profit, greed, and expansion of their territory, while Jesus explains his purpose and motivation in the following text:

Character

The Spirit of the Lord is upon me, for he has anointed me to bring Good News to the poor.

He has sent me to proclaim that captives will be released, that the blind will see, that the oppressed will be set free, and that the time of the Lord's favor has come. Luke 4:18–19 (NLT)

One of the most difficult challenges for believers working in corporate America is the fight to not be contaminated with the negative culture often associated with corporate America (There is a reason why millions go to work every day hating their jobs).

This challenge is greatly exacerbated by the many masks people wear in corporate America. In an effort to climb the corporate ladder, many will cast aside their true identity in favor of joining the ranks of those they believe are rising to the top.

It is a strange irony in our culture that we often find ourselves rooting for the underdog while longing to be with those on top, with the so-called winners, and with those in the corner suite.

Schizophrenic behavior is the driver behind the reason we wear the different masks. We don't want to alienate those with whom we are most comfortable, however, at the same time, we want to demonstrate upward mobility to those in leadership positions of power.

The guys with whom we watch the Sunday game travel in different circles than the guys that watch it from the corporate boxes.

The use of different masks allow us to flow easily between groups, yet we still have the challenge of maintaining our integrity, our honesty, and our truthfulness before the Lord.

We must understand that character is also about leadership and, just as the quote from my eighth grade teacher states, your character is what you do when you think no one is looking. When it comes to leadership, people are evaluating you all the time whether you are aware of it or not.

Legendary player and coach Tony Dungy wrote in his book, *The Mentor Leader*:

> **As their title suggests, mentor leaders seek to have a direct, intentional, and positive impact on those they lead. At its core, mentoring is about building character into the lives of others, modeling and teaching attitudes and behaviors, and creating a constructive legacy to be passed along to future generation of leaders, I don't think it's possible to be an accidental mentor.** (Dungy & Whitaker, 2010)

One must always remember that all of our work should be done unto the Lord, so that we are not inside the organization to become like the organization. Rather, be inside the organization helping the organization to become more like Christ.

Frank Outlaw's often shared quotation is useful for our reading at this point, it reads:

> **"Watch your thoughts, for they become words.**
> **Watch your words, for they become actions.**
> **Watch your actions, for they become habits.**
> **Watch your habits, for they become character.**
> **Watch your character, for it becomes your destiny."**

Your strongest asset is having a good name and a good reputation. Both are determined by how people assess your character, moreover, both are measured, as the earlier quotation stated, by, "what you do when you think no one is looking".

Our lives are not guaranteed to be free of adversity, pain, or guilt. In fact, we are promised that trouble will find its way to our doorstep. The good news for believers is that we have an example of how to handle trouble and live victorious and overcoming lives through Christ.

Jesus said these words:

> **I'm not asking you to take them out of the world, but to keep them safe from the evil one.**
>
> **They do not belong to this world any more than I do.**
>
> **Make them holy by your truth; teach them your word, which is truth.**
>
> **Just as you sent me into the world, I am sending them into the world. John 17:15–18 (NLT)**

What Jesus is saying and praying to God, on behalf of the disciples, the Christians of yesterday, and the believers of today, is that our safety and protection rest in our trusting in the Lord.

It is God who will protect us from the hurt, harm, and danger of the environment in which we find ourselves.

Our responsibility is to trust God and to give him the glory due unto his name.

This, my friend, is a huge challenge for believers in corporate America, but, nevertheless, it is a challenge that God will see us through if we trust him.

It is important that, even in the midst of wrong, we are always found doing what is right. The essence of Jesus's prayer to God on our behalf is that we are always equipped to say and do what is right.

The book of Proverbs is largely credited to King Solomon and his desire to codify some of the lessons he learned and the wisdom imparted to him for future generations. The Bible declares Solomon as the wisest man to have ever lived, so needless to say, a reading of Proverbs is an excellent guide and source of wisdom and instruction for both the believer and nonbeliever working in corporate America.

In Proverbs it reads:

> **"Trust in the Lord with all your heart, and do not rely on your own understanding;**
>
> **Think about him in all your ways and he will guide you on the right path" (Proverbs 3:5–6, NLT).**

In the book of James, we learn that the Lord wants the believers to be wise and have a surplus of wisdom.

In James it states:

> **"If you need wisdom, ask our generous God, and he will give it to you. He will not rebuke you for asking" (James 1:5, NLT).**

In chapter Three, James writes:

> **"But the wisdom from above is first of all pure. It is also peace loving, gentle at all times, and willing to yield to others. It is full of mercy and the fruit of good deeds. It shows no favoritism and is always sincere.**
>
> **And those who are peacemakers will plant seeds of peace and reap a harvest of righteousness"** (James 3:17–18, NLT).

The corporate environment can be full of challenges, turns, and twists. It is one of the reasons why people wear so many different masks trying to navigate their way through this, most challenging, environment.

Some of the twists and turns occur when a colleague, with whom you have shared quality time outside of the office, is surprisingly promoted and becomes your supervisor. Another twist can occur when a previous manager that disagreed with you on many issues is now the CEO of the company. While these are arbitrary examples for this writing, they, and many other twists, can easily alter the trajectory of your career. It is at moments and times such as these that one's faith must be securely anchored. We are to keep our faith always in the Creator and not His creation.

> **"It is better to trust in the Lord than to put confidence in man"** (Psalm 18:8, KJV).

One of the benefits of working in a corporate environment, especially a large one if you choose to avail yourself, is the number of diverse people you will come into contact with that can, hopefully and prayerfully, help in your growth and development. Your engagement with a wide group of individuals helps you to monitor and measure the mountains of information and advice you are certain to receive from coworkers. While some companies have instituted mentor and orientation programs to quick start your acclimation to the company, there is an expectation that you will be a quick study and carrying your own weight in a few weeks.

While the corporation in and of itself can provide great opportunities, and plenty of perks and chances to make a good living. There are also many downsides with respect to the interaction between the individual and the corporation.

Believers must always remember that their first loyalty is to Christ and Christ alone. Therefore, it is incumbent upon the saints to heed the word of God; paraphrasing Joshua we are to meditate on the Word of God day and night and then put the Word into practice.

When we find ourselves challenged or feel we have come face to face with an uncompromising situation we must remember the prayer of the apostle Peter who himself overcame character flaws in his life. Peter wrote:

> **"May God give you more and more grace and peace as you grow in your knowledge of God and Jesus our Lord.**
>
> **By his divine power, God has given us everything we need for living a godly life. We have received all of this by coming to know him, the one who called**

us to himself by means of his marvelous glory and excellence.

And because of his glory and excellence, he has given us great and precious promises. These are the promises that enable you to share his divine nature and escape the world's corruption caused by human desires.

In view of all this, make every effort to respond to God's promises. Supplement your faith with a generous provision of moral excellence, and moral excellence with knowledge, and knowledge with self-control, and self-control with patient endurance, and patient endurance with godliness, and godliness with brotherly affection, and brotherly affection with love for everyone.

The more you grow like this, the more productive and useful you will be in your knowledge of our Lord Jesus Christ" (2 Peter 1:2–8, NLT).

Our character matters. As we traverse the landscape of the corporate world, we should be on the lookout for those individuals who can assist us in strengthening our character.

As I mentioned earlier, Peter—yes, knife wielding, cussing Peter—had character flaws to overcome, and you and I will have our own set of flaws and challenges as well.

Peter, like many of us, had to come to decide which path he would choose. Our character will drive our conscious and subconscious thinking as we contemplate the selections before us.

Choosing the right company can have profound impact on your career, your family, your quality of life, and your community.

Our national sports' franchises give us great insight into the selection process with their celebrated "Draft Days." While fans are excited to see who will be the newest player to join their team, the team owners and coaches are confident their homework and research on the chosen player will return dividends.

Our mindset in choosing which company we lend our talents should also follow a rigorous process that will allow us to make a wise choice.

Choosing your Company

My mother would often instruct me on how I should choose my friends with the words "birds of a feather flock together." I am certain you have either heard those words directly or you know of someone who has; they are part of the "mothers' universal database of things to say to growing children." In all seriousness, mom's words are powerful predictors for our career success and happiness if we do our homework and make wise choices for the "companies" we choose.

The prophet Amos asked a question found in Amos 3:3,

> **"Can two people walk together without agreeing on the direction"? (NLT)**

The direction of our lives and careers is heavily dependent upon our desires and the destinations we choose to pursue.

One of my family's favorite movies is the 1939 classic *The Wizard of Oz*. Many of us are familiar with this great story of how Dorothy, who once believed that she wanted to get away from home, found herself in a very strange land, and with strange people, all as a result of her desire to get away from home.

Worse still, Dorothy comes to realize that she has just committed an offense by killing the wicked witch. Dorothy exclaimed that she did not plan to kill the witch, it was simply the direction of her falling house that fell on the witch that caused her death. To Dorothy's great surprise, her accidental killing of the witch garnered her a welcoming reception complete with applause and song. She had taken away the menace to the people.

Celebrating and acknowledging her hero's welcome, Dorothy nevertheless wanted to return home. Her earlier desire to leave and get away to "any place" brought Dorothy face to face with the consequences of not choosing a desired destination. Dorothy's new location becomes ground zero for her quest to return home to the place she now recognizes as the desire of her heart.

The challenge now before Dorothy, as it is for many in large organizations, is finding out which way is home. Which is the correct path for us to take to reach our desired destiny or destination? To put it another way, which is the path for our success?

Dorothy was given a wonderful parade and ceremony. She was taken to the center of town and was advised that in order to get home, she first needed to get the assistance of the great Wizard of Oz located in the Emerald City.

Dorothy was instructed by her newfound friends that all she needed to reach the Emerald City was to stay on the path of the yellow brick road. "Follow the yellow brick road and you will reach your desired destination" was what she heard.

As we break from our trip down memory lane with Dorothy, we know from life's challenges and situations that it is not always easy to stay on course. Dorothy soon found out that it wasn't easy to stay on course. She encountered obstacles that distracted her and got in the way of her vision of the Emerald City. So it is with us and our desire to successfully achieve our destination in corporate America.

There is a saying, "if you don't know where you are going, any road will get you there." While *The Wizard of Oz* is a wonderful story, the reality for those who fail to choose which companies they will work for and which companies and or industries they will avoid, will cause their career to spin out of control. It will leave them with Dorothy's question swirling in their head, "how did I get here?"

Our most important task is to clearly know our destination and what we are seeking to accomplish with respect to our chosen career. We must be prepared to work through the challenges and the obstacles that might attempt to interrupt our path.

In the case of Dorothy, there were lions and tigers and bears oh my! For you and I, our lion may appear as a lack of skills, a lack of training or a lack of clarity regarding the company. This is where the rigorous research and homework must take place. At times, there may be a mix and match between the culture of the organization and the character of the employee.

There are a variety of obstacles that can come our way as we move closer towards our destination. The key is to be clear and agree on a direction before we start travelling down the career road. Wherever you find yourself today in corporate America, you need a plan, a vision, and a statement of direction to guide your path.

Most organizations spend quality time and dollars to prepare strategic plans in advance. These plans are designed to help steer the organization to their destination: success. Likewise, it is imperative that you as an individual also have a plan that will lead you to success.

The first assignment, for both you and the organization, is to define what success looks like.

Author Bruce Poon TIP the founder of G Adventures, the hugely successful global travel agency, speaks to the need to understand and define what success looks like.

In his book *LoopTail* he writes the following:

> **"The only way to really transcend your product or what you do is to recognize that work has to be about more than work-it has to be about something greater. By transcending the idea of work being just the daily grind, and by engaging the community around you—both customers and employees—to pursue a higher purpose, the Looptail can truly work.**
>
> **In sum, I believe that if businesses want to be both sustainable and successful, they have to infuse their organizations with *passion* and *purpose,* as a way to engage the people *inside* the business, which will in turn engage people outside of it. Today our customers are as amazed by our business model and what we stand for as they are by the quality of our tours. These goals should be at the heart of every business model and are relevant to every industry.**
>
> **It's about "paying it forward" by finding your purpose, and infusing your work and your life with it, you create the conditions for your own success."**
> (Tip Poon, 2013)

Just as one corporation will not allow a competitor to define its success, you must take sole responsibility for defining what success looks like to you. Understand that planning is essential for reaching your goals.

Remember the wisdom Lewis Carroll provided in Alice's Adventure in Wonderland:

"If you don't know where you're going any road will take you there."

You must make certain you understand how the organization defines success as this is immensely critical to your growth, your development, and your internal peace. If your measure of success varies widely from the company's view of success, major adjustments will be required, and you need not guess who will make the adjustments.

As we stated in the introduction corporations are created as self-sustaining entities. This should not come as news or an alarm to anyone working in today's corporate environment however, for those who are determined to maintain your integrity and walk in a way that is pleasing to God you have a responsibility to choose the right environment.

Does this mean you have to walk away from each organization that has a different view of success? Absolutely not. What it means is that your upward mobility may be limited.

As an example if a success criterion for aspiring executives is that they must work in different departments of the company and in different geographic areas of the country to obtain an officer level position then you must be willing to make those adjustments. If it is your desire to stay local, be close to your family, and perhaps work in your ministry, that is a valid choice that needs to be made with integrity and without regret. This can prove a difficult choice for many, however, the believer is comforted by the words of Psalm 75:6–7 (KJV):

> "**For promotion cometh neither from the east, nor from the west, nor from the south.**
>
> **But God is the judge: he putteth down one, and setteth up another**"

Defining and developing your plan for success upfront will place you light years ahead of those without a plan.
Habakkuk 2:2 (KJV)

> "**And the LORD answered me, and said, Write the vision, and make it plain upon tables, that he may run that readeth it.**"

You should know that in your quest to get to the place that you have defined as success there are some things that you must bring to the table. Two critical items you must bring are accountability and responsibility. One must be held accountable and be responsible to the plan if you're going to achieve the success that you desire while remaining in compliance to the rules and regulations of the corporation.

Clarify the Rules

Inside the organization, there are rules and regulations, and it is important that we understand how well we are following the rules. We understand as believers that there is a contentious debate over the difference between law and spirit; however, in corporations there is sometimes a difference between what one says and what he or she does.

The major points of contention in most companies center around the consistent treatment employees receive from their supervisors. Unfortunately, too many individuals have been promoted to leadership ranks without the appropriate training or adequate assessment to determine they are equipped to lead others.

Additionally, there remains a subtle yet present philosophical divide between management and employees that is reminiscent of the ongoing divide between organized labor and corporate management. One of the first things provided to new hires during their orientation process is a handbook of company policies and procedures, complete with specific guidelines on handling disputes with supervisors. While many companies have a vested interest in fair treatment of their employees, others have a culture that provides lip service of fair treatment and creates an opportunity and environment to establish a collective bargaining process.

The argument that some corporations have been putting forth over the last couple of decades in their social responsibility reports is that they have improved the world of work that *our* people are our most important assets. The challenge for the believer is to be able to discern fairly quickly whether or not the words they heard during the recruitment process match up to the culture of the corporation.

This is a serious issue for many people in the world of work. In fact, if you could take a poll, or review the polls already taken, of the millions of people working in the corporate environment, you would find many expressing great dissatisfaction with both their jobs and with their places of employment.

The reasons for this dissatisfaction mostly points back to the fact that the environment was created by those in leadership who possessed a self-serving attitude that fostered a competitive and greed seeking culture. The leadership culture places a higher value on their own jobs, their careers, and their paychecks than the value they place on those who work for them and those who are largely responsible to make the organization successful.

One of the challenges that we have in the world of work today is that corporations believe they have come a long way and they are better at treating individuals such that organized labor is no longer needed. On the contrary organized labor believes that corporations have become so strong that they are essentially doing what they want at the expense of the people working in the organization and a few are getting rich while many are not.

It is an ongoing challenge and the challenge was magnified recently with the economic downturn of 2008 and the global recession. Since 2008 there has been increased emphasis on the economic inequality between workers and CEOs however, I digressed.

Now, before we digressed much further, let us agree that the subject of quality employment practices is in itself worthy of a separate book, so I would just make the point here that it is important for you and I to know the rules and to understand the culture and how that culture either complements or contradicts what we believe God wants us to do with the time he has granted us.

Let's get back to the point of understanding the corporations' position versus labors' position versus where you find yourself in a given organization.

I will share with you an experience that I had in one organization that did not have collective bargaining but they had what was known as an employee support groups. The purpose of the support groups was to bring like-minded employees together to be able to discuss the environment and the world of work. The task of the support groups (managed by the HR department) was to see what adjustments could be made to improve the quality of life in the workplace. The organization supported the groups and encouraged them to meet and share ideas and thoughts to enhance the workplace.

I was asked to lead one of the support groups that I had joined. I had become familiar with several of the individuals and I understood their motivation for being in the support group but more importantly I understood their motivation for asking me to lead it.

Before I would agree to take on the leadership of the organization, I met with them and I told him I had some stipulations and they were our vision and goals must:
- Align with the Corporate Culture.
- Communicate goals for Career Development.
- Create a Community Outreach Initiative.

The overarching theme was to agree that we were a support group and not there to organize a union. I wanted to make it clear to them that our goal was to learn and understand the culture of the organization and find ways to help the organization improve as opposed to organizing against the organization.

I shared with them that I wanted us to identify ways that the organization could help us with career development within the organization; in other words, we were trying to agree and walk in the same direction not go in separate directions.

So, when I came to them with the idea of aligning with corporate culture, identifying career development opportunities, and creating a community outreach project, they understood the direction I wanted to move the support group towards. They agreed and I became the president of the support group

Understand that my reasoning for mentioning this is that alignment must be clear and you must always understand which direction you're traveling.

"Can two people walk together without agreeing on the direction?" (Amos 3:3, NLT)

We must have agreement on the direction with respect to our place of work and employment otherwise we are not aligned and we need to make a different choice

There's another incident I had with respect to organize labor and unions. When I first started work as a young man, I worked for an organized company, which meant that everyone in the company had to be part of the union

I didn't have any bad feelings against the union, however, the union dues were a sizable part of my paycheck. As a young man just beginning in the world of work, I did not understand why I had to pay a certain percentage of my hard-earned money to people I did not know and for reasons that I did not understand.

I was able to work at the job for the first month without having to pay dues, but I learned the power of the union in the second month when I was asked to make a decision to either join the union or to lose my job. Fortunately for me, a new opportunity came before I had to make that decision and I decided to seek employment elsewhere when the new opportunity was presented to me.

I share this story not to suggest in any way shape or form that I do not like unions, I share it to Illustrate that we don't always understand what we are rejecting or accepting, moreover it is important that we are clear and understand the road that we are travelling.

I am certain that the union was very helpful to the people who worked in the organization, but for me as a young a person just coming out of high school, I saw the intrusion into my paycheck and not understanding the value of the union. Paying hefty dues was something that I did not want to participate in at that time.

As my career progressed I began to understand the value and purpose of having a Union to represent and protect workers' rights.

Several decades later I held a non-union "At-Will" position in an organization where I was suddenly released when a CEO whom I had competed against for the top spot was selected to lead the organization. My talents, skills and capabilities notwithstanding, were no match against the "AT-Will policy.

Let me conclude by saying the battle in our country about workers' rights is ongoing and intensifying. There are clearly corporations that value individuals and value the labor provided by their employees; they also understand that there must be a quality of life balance between the workplace and home. Those organizations should be applauded, recognized, and, where possible, duplicated. However, there remains in the workplaces of America too many organizations who only give lip service with regard to caring for the welfare of their employees and fail to improve the quality of work life balance.

Godly leaders must be positioned in the marketplace to influence and decide how best to meet the rights of workers and the needs of the organization. We must continue to be vigilant and challenge each other to create caring environments for all.

The challenge for the believer is to keep the question of Amos ever before them as they move from one organization to the next. Identifying and creating a support system of mentors can prove most helpful in maintaining your course.

Calling All Mentors

Your first priority after joining the organization is to become acquainted with your work assignment, work location and the colleagues in your immediate department. Shortly thereafter, you should begin to identify potential mentors through meetings, luncheons, or corporate activities. Ideally, the mentors will also be believers; however, your first filter is to identify good people who can share with you their experiences regarding the organization's culture.

Your spiritual discernment is key in the identification and selection of your mentors. My mom and those of her generation would often repeat to their children the saying "birds of a feather flock together" as a way of telling us to know and be responsible for the friends we chose to be around.

If our discernment failed, we had the safety net of mom's discernment to direct us away from certain behaviors and personalities. Unless one is extremely fortunate to work in a corporation or a family business, we will no longer have the safety net of mom's discernment when it comes to aligning ourselves with other associates and colleagues in a mentor-mentee relationship.

The good news is that mom's advice regarding the birds' remains applicable when you begin to interview and select or request a mentor.

This is an important decision and one that every successful person will share at some moment in their career that it was the help of their mentors that made them successful.

Take the appropriate time and do your homework!

Finding and working with mentors can prove to be an invaluable addition to your strategic plan and toolkit as you navigate your new environment. It is also an important step in establishing your own "brand".

Mentors can help you navigate the various challenges you may find yourself in as you experience life inside corporate America. It is my sincere hope that you will take seriously the importance of finding, selecting, growing, and learning from your mentors.

"Where no counsel is, the people fall: but in the multitude of counselors there is safety" (Proverbs 11:14, KJV).

I say mentors because it is important that one have a variety or diversity of input before making critical career decisions.

At one time, the idea of seeking a single mentor—the career champion, the godfather—was the goal of the corporate aspirant. In a business world full of minor changes, longevity at one organization where your dad is the major shareholder may yet work.

The reality for the remaining ninety and nine tenths of the working world is to seek as much input as one can humanly process in an effort to map one's desires, talents, skills, and ambitions to an organizational culture.

As you continue to seek out mentor's bear in mind that you may also be in a position to mentor others.

Proverbs 27:17 teaches us that: "As Iron sharpens Iron, so a friend sharpens a friend" (NLT).

We are often caught off guard by the enemy as he wants us to forever be in competition with one another. Working in Corporate America we are constantly confronted with the pressure of peer to peer competition.

The makeup of many corporations is designed to have a few plum jobs offered to the abundance of talented individuals. As a result of the scarcity of titles and great jobs, the focus of adding value, supporting your peers, or working in cooperation as a team is replace by an intense focus on getting promoted.

A focus on self and upward mobility in search of the "almighty" dollar creates an atmosphere of intense competition.

A focus on Self, Satan, and our Society (Materialistic World) is the Devil's attempt to move your focus away from GOD and the plan and purpose God has for your life. Our focus must remain on GOD's goodness and not on Satan's distractions which only serve as a divisive tool creating unhealthy competition.

Unhealthy competition over time weakens and saps the collective strength of the organization. Employees turn their focus to their individual careers and away from adding their unique and Godly given gifts in order to enhance the value of the corporation.

In the introduction of his devotional book *TGIF: Today GOD is First,* author Os Hillman writes:

"When we come to know Christ intimately and understand that God has ordained each of us for a specific purpose, we learn that God desires us

> **to *live out* our purpose (His purpose) through our calling in our spheres of influence and in our work. By living out our calling where we spend most of our time Monday through Friday, we can transform our families, workplaces, communities, cities and nations. May we begin each day declaring, "Today God is First!"** (Hillman, 2007)

I am not suggesting that employees should not focus on their careers; they absolutely should remain in charge of their career. What I am suggesting is that focusing on your career and adding value to the organization is not mutually exclusive. The ability to strike the right balance between your calling (purpose) and your work environment is critical to your success of serving God while serving your community.

Bishop TD Jakes wrote in his "Ten Commandments of Working in a Hostile Environment"

> **"You will never be able to keep what you do right and well a secret."** (Jakes, 2002)

As individuals our challenge remains to strike the right balance of serving God while reporting to our corporate office each day. Our inability to maintain a proper balance can result in failures that can prove to be catastrophic to both our careers and our communities.

One example of the inability of organizations to appreciate the balance of providing service to the community, while still making a respectable profit, was during President George W. Bush's second term.

It was during this period that America begin to witness the cancerous spread of the all-consuming and unbalanced greed of corporate America. Moreover, as the economy quickly sped out of control Americans were not fully able to diagnose the impact of that excessive greed on the US economy.

As a result, millions of Americans lost their jobs, homes, and millions of dollars in wealth, including the retirement savings of many seniors. When the dust settled, we found there were individuals in many organizations that put competition and greed above the desire to make their organizations better by striking a balance between service to the community and making a respectable return.

This is a good place to pause and remind ourselves that while the corporation is a self-sustaining entity, it is run by men and women. Yes, men and women just like you and I.

If the corporation is to be a great entity producing great things for our country, then those great things can and will be traced to the decisions of the women and men who make it so. Conversely when bad things, evil things, and corruption emerges from Corporate America they too can be traced to the decisions, deeds and actions of the Men and Women who lead the corporation.

Apostle John in his epistle 1 John 3:17–18 wrote:

> "[17] **If someone has enough money to live well and sees a brother or sister[f] in need but shows no compassion—how can God's love be in that person?**
>
> [18] **Dear children, let's not merely say that we love each other; let us show the truth by our actions." (NLT)**

This brings me back to the point of this chapter: we need to pray for leadership that is strong and God fearing, like-minded leadership that will sharpen the countenance of each other. These successful men and women who reverence God will seek ways to help and assist their colleagues by working collaboratively to improve the wellbeing of the entire organization.

In far too many organizations and institutions, the idea of networking is reduced to meet and greet gatherings where you can identify potential allies to aid your success. As a result, the focus is not on the person and the building of a relationship, but rather on the accomplishments of the person and how you might benefit from what others have accomplished. The implicit covetousness notwithstanding, this approach is cold, calculating and insincere.

Collaboration requires that you see and value the individual as much as you recognize the value of your gifts. The sharing and blending of each other's' gifts honors and recognizes that "WE" are all made in the image and likeness of God, and we all have gifts to share.

When the focus is on helping others we move away from competition towards cooperation. The best organizations blossom when individuals are regularly rewarded and encouraged to use their talents and capabilities, as well as their roles and their spheres of influence to help other employees succeed. It is the responsibility of the leadership to chart the course for success and provide the tools and framework for the team to work in a collaborative and integrated way.

For example, I once worked in a corporation where I networked with a colleague in government relations and a colleague in shareholder relations. My assignment at the time was in the technology department of the organization.

What made our collaboration so unusual was there was not a need for us at our current levels in our departments to cross lines and collaborate. Each of us could have been successful as a standalone in our respective departments.

Despite the lack of a formal structure for collaboration, the three of us met on a regular basis to share with each other the respective work we were doing in our departments. During our discussions, we sought ways that we might be helpful to one another. To our surprise, we quickly found opportunities to assist each other.

The government relations individual benefited from the technology tools and ideas that allowed her to keep close tabs on all legislation that could potentially impact the organization. The shareholder administrator used the technology ideas to keep a watchful eye on news that could periodically affect stock prices both positively and negatively. The technologist was in a position to continuously learn from both parties regarding how the company's business was done and how ideas in technology could further enable a greater customer experience.

(Note: If you are not clear on how your organization makes money, stop reading and have your mentor explain it to you in language you can both understand and articulate to others.)

The end result was greater productivity for the corporation, as well as additional skills and knowledge being added to the portfolio of each individual working collaboratively and not competitively.

Iron Sharpening Iron.

The ability for us to collaborate was aided by our recognition that our mentors collaborated with other individuals throughout the company and instructed us to do likewise. The mentors were critical in guiding us towards a proper balance and alignment of our gifts and aspirations with the vision and goals of the corporation.

The role of the mentor cannot be overstated; mentors are beneficial to recent graduates just starting their careers, to seasoned executives looking to transition to other companies, and to all of those in the middle of their corporate journey.

Creating Your Brand

As an employee, and as an individual, you are responsible for creating and sustaining your own brand equally and creating value each and every day.

Are you the self-starter? Are you the go-to person when things get challenging? Are you the innovator, the idea person, the closer, the steady manager who will not rock the boat? Whether or not you identify with those descriptors or others is only part of the story. The key is how others in decision-making positions describe you (often behind closed doors).

In the advertising world, brand management is key to a company's survival and long-term success. If their products are not positioned and or perceived in the consumer's mind as top quality products it will be reflected in their sales. What's most interesting is the tactics top companies use to alter the consumer's perception. Tactics such as packaging, pricing, product naming, and the constant refrain of "new and improved".

The next time you reach for a particular product in the supermarket, stop for a moment and ask yourself, "Why am I purchasing this particular brand?" As you contemplate the answer, know that questions are asked in the same fashion that affect individual careers.

Your brand management is vitally essential to growing and managing your corporate career.

Organizations big and small manage their work products through the use of departments, projects, and functional teams. Despite the complexity of the organization, you are responsible for identifying your place in the organization's value chain where your skills, your work, and your time intersect and add value each day.

You must understand and embrace the concepts of continuous improvement and continuous learning in an effort to steadily contribute to your growth and development, while simultaneously creating value for the organization. Having a working knowledge of project management principles and the effective and efficient use of time, resources, and dollars—in others words, knowing how to be a "good steward"—is a big plus.

Additionally, you must understand how teamwork, accountability, and responsibility are viewed from the perspective of the organization's leadership team; in essence, from the eyes of those in charge of the organization. When presented with the opportunity to demonstrate your ability to handle larger assignments, you must be prepared to show immediate success, or, as the saying goes, "hit the ground running."

For example, in one organization I had the task of building a small team to provide software installation and technical service to customers throughout the country. Though my team was mostly inherited (meaning I did not get the chance to hire, shape, and mold them according to my management style), I was able to add a few individuals to compliment the team.

One of the first things that we did as a group was to go off-site and to establish how we would work. We were planning our work and we wanted to make sure that we understood what was needed to be done. Our goal was to create a great customer experience for every customer interaction we had. We wanted to provide flawless execution of the work that was required to be done. We looked for models that we could replicate and one of the models that we wanted to utilize was the model of IBM's customer and service engineer.

Those models were important to us because IBM had perfected the way of speaking technology from the business person's viewpoint, and not from the technologist's viewpoint. In other words, IBM engineers were trained to listen and hear what the customer was communicating. This allowed IBM to create an environment that kept the customer in control of the decision. Technology was being installed to support the business goals not simply to secure a technology purchase.

The IBM service and customer engineers took the extra step to make sure they understood the business, and then they were able to explain to the customer how the technology would help meet or exceed the business goals.

To use that model, we also spent time identifying the service area and the service criteria. We assembled "rules of engagement" that we called "the basic instructions" before leaving the environment. In other words, it was our Bible, and we wanted to make sure that we were clear that all these things were done in a decent and orderly fashion before we left the customers environment.

Additionally, to create a complete guide to serving the customers and creating a great customer experience, we felt it necessary to bring all of the individual stakeholders together. We took the time to interview each one of them from the standpoint of asking and learning how best can we "serve you as you serve your customer."

In a very real sense, we made a clear distinction between the consumer and the customer by recognizing the customer's care and the customer experience ultimately belonged to the stakeholder. Though we had custodial responsibilities and custody was temporal, our goal was simply defined as "creating a great customer experience" for both the consumer and the stakeholder.

I point this out because we spent the better part of two days just listening and learning about the motivation of our stakeholders as it relates to their customers. Securing stakeholder input and understanding their approach towards their customers resulted in our group being viewed as wildly successful in the eyes of both the consumer and the stakeholders. We listened for the motivation and we built our execution around what the stakeholder (our customer) deemed most important. Our critical question of how best can we serve you allowed us to create:

- A great customer experience.
- A powerful first impression.
- A focus on their business.
- A culture of character and integrity.

It is imperative that you understand the culture of the organization and, if possible, the prioritization of the values of the organization and what is required to be successful in that particular corporation.

Perhaps you have heard the famous quote: "The operation was a success, but the patient died." Or "we completed the project on time and we have twenty original team members remaining out of two hundred." Translation: the project managers killed off 180 staff members to complete the task. These are examples of incorrectly prioritizing one's values. Understanding what a company says it values are, and how the values are prioritized, can make a world of difference in navigating your career.

One final example of prioritizing values took place several decades ago, after the death of seven individuals in Chicago was traced to Tylenol pills that had been tampered with and laced with poison. The manufacturer Johnson & Johnson was faced with the massive recall and the expense of removing every bottle of Tylenol from the shelves in the city of Chicago.

The company mission statement was to first protect consumers and medical professionals using their products. Based on the priority of its values, the company made the decision to remove every bottle of Tylenol throughout the country.

> **"Our Credo challenges us to put the needs and well-being of the people we serve *first*.**
>
> **Robert Wood Johnson, former chairman from 1932 to 1963 and a member of the Company's founding family, crafted Our Credo himself in 1943, just before Johnson & Johnson became a publicly traded company. This was long before anyone ever heard the term "corporate social responsibility." Our Credo is more than just a moral compass. We believe it's a recipe for business success. The fact that Johnson & Johnson is one of only a handful of companies that have flourished through more than a century of change is proof of that."** (Johnson & Johnson, 2016)

Branding is indeed important, and as you can see from the Johnson and Johnson case, the entire nation was watching and acknowledging their response. While our individual careers may never match the size and scope of Johnson & Johnson, our reputation is equally important to our success.

Our success as individuals in the building of our brand requires us to extend our exposure beyond the project team or department we are initially assigned when we join the organization. Many individuals mistakenly limit their accountability to their direct supervisor, however, to be successful in navigating the organization, you must look beyond your direct supervisor. You must look to your department head and to the group department head, if one exists in your organizational structure. In doing so, it is key that your direct supervisor is secure in their job and not at all threatened by your talent and skill. An insecure supervisor is a cancer in the life of your career; avoid them at all cost. A secure supervisor is one that is interested in helping your career and will look for opportunities to expose your talents to others in the organization.

Creating and Adding Value

I want to underscore the importance of aligning your mission with the mission of the organization. It is imperative that we understand how the organization is attempting to implement its goals and business metrics; in other words, how are they going to measure their success.

Our task is also to do an assessment of our individual goals, skills, and talents. To add value, we must discern how we will align our gifts, talents, and skills with the mission of the organization. More importantly, we must actively develop, enhance, and increase our value to the corporation. We must actively stay abreast of new systems, new technologies, and new strategies to position both the firm and ourselves for greater success.

Please understand that the organizations' need and requirements for skills and talent does not equate to the organization needing *you*. The organization is after the value you possess.

As long as the firm is extracting value, or the firm continues to perceive you have value, you will remain on the payroll. If the value proposition becomes negative, you will be removed from the organization. Staying focused on the value you bring not only helps to keep you ahead of the proverbial pink slip, corporate restructure, or downsizing, it also helps you stay aware of your market value in the larger industry.

Author Stephen Covey wrote in his book *Principle-Centered Leadership*:

> **"When we continue our education, our economic security is not as dependent upon our jobs, our bosses' opinion, or human institutions as it is upon our ability to produce. The great unseen job market is called " unsolved problems," and there are always many vacancies for those who exercise initiative and learn how to create value for themselves by showing how they essentially represent solutions to these problems."** (Covey, 1990)

Knowing your value requires honesty, integrity, and discipline on your part. This is not simply a case of reviewing your résumé or simple resting on your laurels.

Author and researcher Ines Temple writes that there are four key points we must cultivate if we desire to add value:
1. Have a clear idea of the value we add.
2. Always remain up to date on the latest trends and technology.
3. Being bilingual and having international personal or business experience.
4. Demonstrating energy, enthusiasm, and passion.

> **"We are not paid to go to work—we are paid to add value. It is important that we clearly understand that we are paid to drive achievements, add**

value, and contribute to results. Many believe that our accomplishments serve as *fillers* within our portfolio, but this is not the case. We need to be conscious of what we are doing and how we are contributing to justify our salary. We don't get paid to show up or occupy space, and we are most certainly not getting paid *just because*." (Ines, 2016)

It is critically important during the review or assessment period that you remain clear on your own internal motivations. During the assessment process you must not compromise your character, nor lose your integrity. As hired hands and minds, we need to be absolutely clear and think about our aspirations, dreams, and desires. We need to be clear on what we are providing and what we are receiving in return. When it comes to our character and integrity, we want to be crystal clear at all times. We must seek the alignment King David sought. In Psalm 19:14, David asked God to allow the words of his mouth and the meditation of his heart to be acceptable in God's sight.

> **"May the words of my mouth and the meditation of my heart be pleasing to you, O LORD, my rock and my redeemer" (NLT).**

In other words, David understood that his ultimate supervisor was God and all of his work would be performed under the watchful eye of his creator. David wanted first to align with God and the purpose that God had for his life.

In our materialistic world, we often fail to put God first in our thoughts, and as a result, many will spend years if not decades serving the corporate world only to end up with a major misalignment between their accomplishments and their joy or happiness. Survey after survey shows a large percentage of workers dislike their places of employment and their employers. They work to maintain a lifestyle they have become accustom to over the years and they require the weekly or biweekly paycheck to continue their lifestyle.

Those who are like David—able to align themselves and their thoughts with God's will and purpose for their lives—are better positioned to avoid the bondage of materialism and the trapped feeling of being tied to the corporate entity. This sense of bondage is greatly exacerbated during times of prolonged economic downturns.

If we are not careful, any work or assignment can turn dull, become routine, boring, or simply less challenging over time. We should not exacerbate the situation by choosing a job simply for what it pays and the material things we can purchase. Working to pay for stuff rather than working to live out one's passion is the result of aligning oneself with money rather than aligning yourself with God's purpose for your life.

It is an example of what Jesus said to his disciple's in Matthew 6:24

> ***"No one can serve two masters. For you will hate one and love the other; you will be devoted to one and despise the other. You cannot serve God and be enslaved to money"(NLT).***

This is an important concept for us to learn and put into practice. Those of us who began serving money and materialism can reverse course and acknowledge our work should be unto the Lord and not for the love of money and material things. God is not against us having things; He is against things having control over our decisions and desires.

We are told in Matthew 6:30–34

> **"And if God cares so wonderfully for wildflowers that are here today and thrown into the fire tomorrow, he will certainly care for you. Why do you have so little faith?**
>
> **"So don't worry about these things, saying, 'What will we eat? What will we drink? What will we wear?'**
>
> **These things dominate the thoughts of unbelievers, but your heavenly Father already knows all your needs.**
>
> **Seek the Kingdom of God above all else, and live righteously, and he will give you everything you need.**
>
> **[34] So don't worry about tomorrow, for tomorrow will bring its own worries. Today's trouble is enough for today"** (NLT).

We are cautioned against worrying about things and encouraged to focus on God's kingdom and his character. God promises to provide the things we need when we keep our focus and thoughts on Him.

> **Paul says in Philippians 4:8**
> **"And now, dear brothers and sisters, one final thing. Fix your thoughts on what is true, and honorable, and right, and pure, and lovely, and admirable. Think about things that are excellent and worthy of praise" (NLT).**

Finally, as we seek to create and add value, we must see ourselves as influencers or implementers, but never isolationists. There are things that we must get done in the organization as part of our own self-development, and things we must do to establish key relationships. We will not be successful in any organization, nor in any community, if we act like isolationists. We must learn to integrate our ideas, thoughts, aspirations, and goals into the larger goals of the organization.

Adding value must also be quantified. We can't just state it—we must be able to show it. Working collaboratively as a functional team is a great way to quantify the value. We should avoid the common trap of comparing ourselves with those who are around us rather than comparing ourselves against the standards that we set for ourselves. Our comparison should measure the utilization of the gifts that we have and how those gifts are being used on behalf of the organization.

Proper measurement and utilization of our gifts is also a challenge for those of us in the body of Christ. God has given all of us gifts to use and those gifts are to be celebrated and used for the unity and the edification of the entire body.

> **"In his grace, God has given us different gifts for doing certain things well"** (Romans 12:6, NLT).

Each and every one of us has the ability to add value to our organization. When we focus on the gift God has provided us and share the gift with others, we are not just adding value, we are also celebrating the Giver of our Gifts.

Celebrate the Giver by sharing your Gifts

Every good gift and every perfect gift is from above, and cometh down from the Father of lights, with whom is no variableness, neither shadow of turning. James 1:17 (KJV)

Celebrating the giver may take different forms and styles depending on one's preference and perspective.

Many readers may choose to speculate about the placement of this chapter in the book. Some of my secular friends may suggest that this chapter should be at the end of the book, that it should be the closing thought for the reader as they turn the last pages of the book. My spiritual friends may think that this absolutely must be the first chapter of the book insisting without God nothing at all would exist and I am not one to disagree with that assertion.

I placed this chapter here for no other reason than this discussion should definitely be included in the book in concert with all the other chapters in the book. The placement notwithstanding, we should be mindful of Paul's instruction to the people of Thessalonica and

David's declaration in Psalm 34: We should pray without ceasing and We should bless the Lord at all times.

As we discussed in the previous chapter God has given each of us gifts to utilize for His Glory and His Kingdom. We will explore those verses found in Romans in more detail.

> "**In his grace, God has given us different gifts for doing certain things well. So if God has given you the ability to prophesy, speak out with as much faith as God has given you.**
>
> **If your gift is serving others, serve them well. If you are a teacher, teach well.**
>
> **If your gift is to encourage others, be encouraging. If it is giving, give generously. If God has given you leadership ability, take the responsibility seriously. And if you have a gift for showing kindness to others, do it gladly.**
>
> **Don't just pretend to love others. Really love them. Hate what is wrong. Hold tightly to what is good.**
>
> **Love each other with genuine affection, and take delight in honoring each other.**
>
> **Never be lazy, but work hard and serve the Lord enthusiastically.**

Rejoice in our confident hope. Be patient in trouble, and keep on praying" Romans 12:6–12 (NLT)

We must be reminded that it is the Lord's granting of continued grace in our lives that enables us to navigate the dark challenges of this world's systems.

Our celebrating God need only be dependent on our experiences with him and what he has done in our lives and the lives of those we love.

Nothing celebrates God more than the using of one's gift in the service of God's people and his kingdom.

Eleanor Powell wrote:

> "What we are is God's gift to us.
> What we become is our gift to God."

We become by celebrating the Giver of our gifts. Apostle Paul on a missionary Journey spoke to the people of Athens Greece who were enamored with the idea of GOD and equally enamored with their own intellect and thoughts about GOD.

The Athenians according to Paul had built several altars to worship several gods and to be certain they did not leave room for error by worshipping the wrong god. Paul said they had created an Altar to the "Unknown" God.

It was at their intersection of worship and ignorance (lack of Knowledge) that Paul would meet them and share with them that they could actually know God.

"So Paul, standing before the council, addressed them as follows: "Men of Athens, I notice that you are very religious in every way, for as I was walking along I saw your many shrines. And one of your altars had this inscription on it: 'To an Unknown God.' This God, whom you worship without knowing, is the one I'm telling you about.

He is the God who made the world and everything in it. Since he is Lord of heaven and earth, he doesn't live in man-made temples, and human hands can't serve his needs—for he has no needs. He himself gives life and breath to everything, and he satisfies every need. From one man he created all the nations throughout the whole earth. He decided beforehand when they should rise and fall, and he determined their boundaries.

His purpose was for the nations to seek after God and perhaps feel their way toward him and find him—though he is not far from any one of us.

For in him we live and move and exist. As some of your own poets have said, 'We are his offspring.'

And since this is true, we shouldn't think of God as an idol designed by craftsmen from gold or silver or stone.

God overlooked people's ignorance about these things in earlier times, but now he commands everyone everywhere to repent of their sins and turn to him" (ACTS 17:22–30, NLT).

As we consume our life's' allotted hours in the work environment it is essential we remain cognizant of our gifts, our value and our creator. The hour will arrive for everyone who stands behind an id-badge, a title or a corporate name to come from behind the corporate covering. Those who were able to celebrate and remember:

"Whatever you do, work at it with all your heart, as working for the Lord, not for men, since you know that you will receive an inheritance from the Lord as a reward. It is the Lord Christ you are serving" (Colossians 3:23–24).

Will be able to enjoy the journey.

In other words, when we focus on the "Giver" of our Gifts and His purpose and plan for giving us the Gift, the world will have to stop and take notice of how God is working through us demonstrating his 'Gift' in the earth.

You and I are the conduit, the vessels and the vehicles used for God's glory.

We do not want to find ourselves living like King Saul, who abused his Gift and lost the favor of God over his life. Saul's disobedience to God's command led to his being rejected by God and he no longer was a vessel God could use.

Then Saul admitted to Samuel, "Yes, I have sinned. I have disobeyed your instructions and the Lord's command, for I was afraid of the people and did what they demanded.

But now, please forgive my sin and come back with me so that I may worship the Lord."

But Samuel replied, "I will not go back with you! Since you have rejected the Lord's command, he has rejected you as king of Israel" (1 Sam 15:24–26, NLT).

Our first responsibility is to celebrate and honor the lord, who is the giver and the sustainer of life. Celebrate God and thank him for what he has done, and is doing, in your life.

God is our Source; all else is a resource. Celebrate the Giver.

Culture and Organizational Change

A common thread that runs though most organizations is their propensity to have recurring restructures and realignments. Throughout my experiences beginning in the early 70's and continuing up to the present (2016) regardless of industry, geography, size and net worth; organizations continue to restructure.

Some of the change is driven by competition and the ongoing challenge to maintain and or grow market share. At times change and organizational restructuring is driven by the desire to enter new markets. Over the past several decades' massive change and restructuring was ushered into the corporate environment by technology and innovation.

Todays' millennials many who are adept at using the latest technologies (smartphone, tablets, smartwatches) and social media platforms were only entering grade school when these inventions were still ideas or just breaking into the marketplace.

When we take a closer look at the technology explosion we will discover that our world has experienced more technology growth during the years 1980 -2015 than from the preceding years of 1880 to 1980.

A major hurdle for individuals and companies during transitions of explosive change is the ability to harness and benefit from the changes. Having a corporate culture that embraces change while empowering employees to grow and develop can make the difference between good companies and great companies.

Author Jim Collins in his best-seller *Good to Great* outlined a framework for a successful transition to greatness. Collins shared that we must first get the right people on the bus. "Disciplined-People-Disciplined-Thought will lead to disciplined action or a culture of Discipline."

One of the challenges we have in organizations is trying to mesh our experiences or should I say align our experiences in life with the culture of the organization only to find that our experience appears to be contrary to the organization's culture.

Collins admonition to companies to get the right people on the bus is equally insightful and instructive for the employee to wait for the right bus before boarding.

There are numerous studies and books written on organizations and change, change management systems, organizational dynamics and organizational culture.

Author Edgar Schein who is considered a founder of the field of organizational psychology and has done extensive work in the area of culture and organizational dynamics coined the phrase:

> **"Leadership and Culture Are Two sides of the same Coin"**

Schein wanted corporate leaders to know and understand that culture was not a product that one purchases or a quick fix concept one can implement in order to create a transformative process in the organization. There are three levels of culture according to Schein that move from the very visible to the very tacit and invisible and organizations must deal with all three.

The levels are identified as Artifacts-Espoused Values and Basic Underlying Assumptions. All three matter when attempting to understand the drivers and resisters of change in the environment.

> **"Culture matters because it is a powerful, latent, and often unconscious set of forces that determine both our individual and collective behavior, ways of perceiving, thought patterns, and values.**
>
> **Organizational culture in particular matters because cultural elements determine strategy, goals, and modes of operating.**
>
> **The values and thought patterns of leaders and senior managers are partially determined by their own cultural backgrounds and their shared experience. If we want to make organizations more efficient and effective, then we must understand the role that culture plays and organizational life."**
> (Schein, 1999)

Transformative change is the result of leaders understanding that culture must be taken seriously for it is the culture created by organizations that guide the thinking and behavior of the employees.

Why does this matter to you as an individual attempting to navigate your way to success in the organization? As stated earlier in the Book-It is important that you as an employee give considerable time and energy to understand the culture of your organization in order to determine if the culture complements or conflicts with your character and values.

You may be thinking it is difficult to determine the culture from the outside and for the most part that is a true statement. What you do have at your disposal is the Power of the question. Your ability to ask insightful and penetrating questions upfront during the interview and recruiting process will prove insightful and helpful in researching the culture of the organization.

My undergraduate studies in history required a fair amount of research in an effort to understand the reasoning behind the choices and decisions made by individuals, leaders of corporations and the leaders of sovereign countries.

I can remember and almost hear my professor reminding us that:

"History does not repeat itself-but rather people repeat the mistakes of history"

He would also caution us to learn the power of the question by stating if you can properly frame the question you are halfway to the answer.

This is valuable information to the applicant preparing for their interview. The more you are prepared to ask insightful and penetrating questions regarding the history, behavior, practices and culture of the organization the better are your chances of making an informed decision regarding the accepting or rejecting of their offer.

John Maxwell talks about the power of questions in his book *Good Leaders Ask Great Questions*. He writes:

> **"If you want to be successful and reach your leadership potential, you need to embrace asking questions as a lifestyle."**

I agree with Maxwell and I must share with you that not all corporate environments are open to embracing questions as a lifestyle which is why the interview process is so critical to your ultimate success.

Before you agree to join any organization you have a responsibility to interview them and learn about their leadership. It is during the interview process that HR can be most helpful to you.

However, you must ask the direct questions regarding the environment, the leadership, the challenges, the attrition rate, the number of restructures in the past three–five years, how long do people stay in the job before being promoted, where are the examples of successful employees, where are the examples of those who did not adapt.

It is during the interview process that you must gather all pertinent data to make sure the organization is aligned in the direction you desire your career to go.

In developing your questions, you should structure them around the things that are most important to you and your family.

Think about what is important to you and your family.

Think about your core values.

Think about your walk with Christ

Think about the legacy you want to create

Think about your Character

Think about your reputation

Then pray and ask GOD to help you prepare a series of questions that will bring you clarity whether are not there is alignment between you and the corporation.

Connecting the Dots

"The blessing of the LORD, it maketh rich, and he addeth no sorrow with it" (Proverbs 10:22, KJV).

As we conclude our talk on corporate America and the essential tools needed to successfully navigate the environment I want us to zero in on three key capabilities and competencies. It is imperative that believers develop these capabilities and keep them in use at all times

These capabilities are Focus-Discipline and Relationships. They are essential to the successful navigation of the corporate environment.

With respect to focus Apostle Paul would say in Philippians 3:13–14

"Brethren, I count not myself to have apprehended: but this one thing I do, forgetting those things which are behind, and reaching forth unto those things which are before,

I press toward the mark for the prize of the high calling of God in Christ Jesus" (KJV).

The writer of Hebrews would say:

"And let us run with endurance the race God has set before us. We do this by keeping our eyes on Jesus, the champion who initiates and perfects our faith.[a] **Because of the joy awaiting him, he endured the cross, disregarding its shame. Now he is seated in the place of honor beside God's throne"** **(Hebrews 12:1-2, NLT).**

Clearly we see that focus and discipline is essential to our success. Our focus must be firmly established at the beginning of our interest in any corporation. When we acknowledge all of our work is unto the Lord; when we acknowledge that it is the Lord who gives us the ability to get wealth, when we acknowledge that every good and perfect gift comes from GOD our ability to stay focused is tremendously enhanced.

We are able to avoid the distractions of the world and complete the assignment God has placed before us.

The challenge for most employees is their initial focus is on landing a job, getting a paycheck, paying back school loans if they are recently graduated or paying off the bills and debts one has accumulated if they have been in the workforce for a while.

Unfocused employees are a great advantage to corporations as they can shape, mold and utilize your lack of clarity and focus towards their benefit.

The key to success is knowing what it is that your attempting to achieve on the front end; knowing your value (skills, talents and gifts) and being clear on the mission and motivations (culture) of the corporation.

One writer put it this way: "if you don't know where you're going any road will take you there" So it is with your career in corporate America you must remain focused on what it is you're working to accomplish and how you expect to execute your goals.

The believer's essential ingredient for success is to remember who they are and whose they are. In the Kingdom we understand that the career, the job, the corporation, is not our source of success; it is simply a resource provided by the Lord for you to achieve the things that you are destined to achieve. Proverbs 10:22 reminds us:

"The blessing of the LORD, it maketh rich, and he addeth no sorrow with it" (KJV).

Our goal at all times is to focus on the Lord as our source and to believe with all our heart and mind that he is our only source. When we understand the gifts that are deposited in us from the Lord, and we utilize those gifts in the service of others, we demonstrate to the Lord that our trust is in him—not in a paycheck.

To be clear, the corporate environment can—and at times, does—provide great opportunities to utilize and develop the gifts and the skills that God has blessed you with. We are to utilize those gifts to glorify GOD and not simply for the profit of the organization or for our own selfish greed.

Herein lies the dilemma, the trap. Herein lies the hand of the enemy attempting to steer you off course and to get you thinking selfishly about how you might be successful, achieve the corner suite, achieve monetary success far and above your friends, your neighbors, your family, and all those that you *think* you are competing against.

We are taught in Scripture that we are not to compare ourselves with ourselves; our standard is Christ Jesus and the work that we do we do it not for our own glory. At all times, and in all situations, believers are to work as if we are always working for the Lord.

Many of us desire the ability and the knowledge to achieve what we think is best for our lives and our families. Staying focused early in your career, while it may prove to be a challenge, will certainly keep you doing what the Lord has purposed you to do. Staying focused will keep your mind on Christ and minimize the worldly distractions that are constantly vying for your attention. A disciplined prayer life is the single most critical element in navigating life—especially a life inside corporate America.

Proverbs 3:5–6 is most helpful in underscoring the point of having a disciplined prayer life.

> **"Trust in the Lord with all your heart; do not depend on your own understanding. Seek his will in all you do, and he will show you which path to take" (NLT).**

The entire book of proverbs provides us with answers regarding how to please God and receive our heart's desire.

> **"And we are confident that he hears us whenever we ask for anything that pleases him. And since we know he hears us when we make our requests, we also know that he will give us what we ask for" (1 John 5:14–15, NLT).**

A former colleague of mine was rising rapidly in the corporate world and was given greater authority with each success. While we marveled at his ability to navigate a very political and treacherous environment (it was often said "they eat their young here"), we never quite understood how he always seemed to come out on top. Yes, he worked hard, arrived early, stayed late, and was always ready to tackle the biggest challenge. These were his traits and the traits of his peers; yet, somehow, this individual kept rising to the top. Years later, we learned this individual had a disciplined prayer life. He always took time out to pray.

Those of us on his team didn't see him pray, and we certainly didn't realize that he was praying on a regular basis. Our discovery came when his secretary went into his office and caught him on his knees praying. She did not realize when she stepped away from her desk that he had returned early from a meeting. When she entered his office thinking he was still at the meeting, she witnessed him praying.

When she shared her excitement of seeing the supervisor pray, we learned the secret of his success; he had a disciplined prayer life. He led the organization with prayer and with a focus on how he could serve Christ. The benefit was he built a strong organization with one success after another.

Discipline is essential for your success. It is imperative at the outset that you define what success looks like; it is also imperative at the outset that you work with your supervisor and to the extent possible your supervisor's manager and collectively define what success looks like for you in that corporate environment.

When success is defined, the next step is to determine how you will work together to achieve that success. The final step is to determine how your individual contributions will be measured and rated against the contributions of the whole.

Most organizations have what they call a performance management system in place. It is a systematic review processes put in place by the organization to assist in objectively reviewing and valuing each employee's individual contribution to the whole.

While these systems are well intended they still remain subjective tools for the HR department and the hiring manager. If your organization has such a system in place you have heard the caveat "our performance rating and monetary (merit) increase are not linked"

The reason the system is in place is twofold:

1. the corporation must be in compliance with local-state and federal employment laws regarding fair treatment, being able to cite a universal rating systems for all helps mitigate challenges of unfairness.
2. The organization uses the system as a way to systematically weed out the employees they no longer desire to keep on the payroll.

When the language changes dramatically in your review it is a signal you are headed for a promotion or an exit review. If you aren't clearly taking charge of your career, you will have minimum recourse when they ask you to leave the organization.

It has been my experience in several organizations both for-profit and not-for-profit that the management team often lacks integrity when it comes to maintaining a solid objective performance system.

The writing of the performance goals, objectives, measurements and reviews is often inconsistent across the employee population.

The timing of the performance reviews and the delivery of the performance reviews across all positions also remains inconsistent.

There is a reason why the courts are full of lawsuits and EEOC filings.

Your ability to navigate the performance management system in your favor will greatly depend on how effectively you establish and build relationships throughout the organization. Your successful relationship with both the management team and the HR department are essential for smooth sailing in the organization.

Your HR department must always be aware of your contributions and the value you bring to the organization. Having an ally and an advocate in HR early in your career is most helpful. More importantly, if you develop a relationship where HR can call on you to speak during employee orientation sessions or HR led training programs you will have created a very strong bond and one that can prove helpful especially during times of major organization restructures.

Strong bonds are important in our careers, our homes, our cities and our places of worship. As a student of history I am amazed at our increasing inability to have dialogue and create meaningful relationships across a diverse range of individuals. It appears in our country that despite all of the talk about diversity and inclusion, many Americans,' at the end of the day continue to retreat to their own 'ethnic enclaves

Dr. King's circa 1960 comment that 11Am Sunday Morning was perhaps the most segregated hour in America still rings true almost a half century after he first made the remark.

Corporate America for many presented the best opportunity to get to know and learn of people from diverse backgrounds. A time where individuals would spend a third or more of each day side by side is a perfect place to establish and build great relationships.

Unfortunately, far too many individuals waste time in frivolous corporate competition and fail to truly learn about the wonderful things each share in common.

When we think of building relationships our guide should be the command "Love Thy Neighbor as Thyself." When we treat others as we wish to be treated we are not only building relationships we are also improving the quality of life in the work environment.

As stated earlier one of the clarifying questions you as a candidate want answered before you accept the position is "what type of environment exists in this company." As an individual and a believer, it is important for you to discern that there are some organizations you do not want to be a part of regardless of how much they are willing to pay or how strongly they recruit you.

Every corporation has its own culture that consistently functions and operates regardless of your race, your creed, your gender, your beliefs or your station in life.

It is true in America that the majority of corporate CEOs belong to a single ethnic group. It is also true that the majority of political leaders in America belong to the same ethnic group. It is also true that the majority of pastors in America belong to a single ethnic group. These statistics notwithstanding; the godly person with discernment, focus, a disciplined prayer life, and the ability to build relationships can navigate the murky waters and have a successful career in corporate America.

Community is Still Possible

Today's corporate environment is under severe criticism and attack for its continuous focus on greed and profit at the expense of employees, citizens, communities, and even countries.

As of this writing, America is bracing for a bitter presidential election campaign of 2016. The involvement of corporate sponsorship and the cry for campaign finance reform has taken center stage as voters attempt to align dollars spent with agreeing with the policies and ideas of the candidate. Moreover, the growing wealth inequality that has CEO's earning 300 to 400 times the earnings of workers on the front lines. Lastly, The Supreme Courts' 2011 decision to acknowledge corporations as people has exacerbated the hatred and mistrust of the corporate entity.

Many organizations in the hope of reversing the negative images and stereotypes of the corporation have instituted a "Corporate Social Responsibility" handbook complete with guidelines, policies and procedures.

It is abundantly evident that American Corporations and workers are at a crossroads and a voice of reconciliation is needed to redirect the current destructive and chaotic path towards a more constructive and community centered path.

Christ-centered change agents are needed in greater numbers now than perhaps at any other time in our Nations' history.

Christians in corporate America can be the catalyst for real and genuine change if we choose to keep our conscious minds focused on Christ.

> **"Therefore, since we are surrounded by such a huge crowd of witnesses to the life of faith, let us strip off every weight that slows us down, especially the sin that so easily trips us up. And let us run with endurance the race God has set before us. We do this by keeping our eyes on Jesus, the champion who initiates and perfects our faith. Because of the joy awaiting him, he endured the cross, disregarding its shame. Now he is seated in the place of honor beside God's throne" (Hebrews 12:1–2, NLT).**

Dr. Martin Luther King Jr. kept his eyes on Christ and the belief that we are all made in the Image of God. King perhaps more than any other American during his lifetime understood America's dichotomy between the glorious promises of a United States of America working together in pursuit of happiness and the powerful practices of Individual States pursuing segregation and self-righteousness.

Dr. King's stance against poverty, materialism and militarism is as relevant today as it was during the height of the modern day civil rights movement in the 1960s.

Author Harry C. Boyte, who worked for Dr. Martin Luther King as a teenager in the 1960s, wrote the following in his book *Community IS Possible* about Dr. King as a change agent:

"King's dream might be termed democratic and populist. It held forth the hope that ordinary people could take their lives in their own hands. It affirmed the dignity of a great pluralism of heritages and communities-even those of southern segregationist, faith in whose redemption, and positive features, King never abandoned.

And it grounded a vision of change in our nation's finest traditions and values, the strands he believed offered an alternative possibility to bigotry, unbridled individualism, greed and violence.

Martin Luther King's call to "make democracy real in America" embodied, in sum, the best insight of American populism: the understanding that we are joined by our common wealth, those public purposes and values which express the common threads of our history and our common aspirations for the future, alike.

Indeed, in America's democratic movements, from the Revolution through the great struggles of blacks, women, farmers and workers for dignity and justice, the vocabulary of the commonwealth has reappeared again and again.

It symbolizes a public sphere which simultaneously reflects and reinforces the virtues of individual

citizens, joined in communities conscious of their moral interdependence." (Boyte, 1984)

As I bring this book to a close, I wanted to share with the reader a view of why Dr. King was one of America's greatest agents for change.

Your journey through corporate America will no doubt present you with a myriad of conflicts, crisis, and challenges that you must confront. How you choose to confront the challenges will often reveal more about the strength of you as a person than the complexity or size of the challenge before you.

In the book Lead Like Jesus the author's write:

> **"We live in a world that fuels the fires of pride and fear. Through fads, fashion, and pressure to acquire more and better goods and services, we are constantly being Lured into believing we can secure a sense of meaning and safety.**
>
> **Standing in absolute contrast to these temporary, always at-risk, never secure places to put our trust are the unconditional love and promises of God. Only in a relationship with God can we find and be assured of a never-ending supply of what we need to live and lead as Jesus would."** (Blanchard & Hodges, 2005)

As a follower of Christ, Dr. Martin Luther King Jr. remains one of America's greatest change agents. Though he never worked in corporate America, his sense of community, fairness, and justice for all was, at times, directed to the individuals who managed the corporate environment. Dr. King celebrated and used his gifts in an effort to make our country a better community for all.

He was raised in a middle class southern home and was an exceptional student. He earned his Ph.D. in his mid-twenties, more significantly, as a fourth generation "preacher", Dr. King had the choice of pastoring in both the North and the South at the age of twenty-six.

The world is better today because of the choice Dr. and Mrs. King made. Their choice favored the South as that is where Dr. King believed he could be most helpful. His instincts were correct; he was quickly enthralled in a major undertaking. The twenty-six-year-old pastor was asked in 1955 to lead the initiative, boycotting the Montgomery, Alabama segregated bus system.

It was during this initiative that we first witness the mix of Dr. King's educational depth, preaching preparedness, leadership, organizational skills, and values. His moral compass directed his energies towards freedom, justice, and equality for all, especially for the Negroes in America.

This was no small task. The country was just ninety-two years past the emancipation proclamation that ended slavery. However, the country, particularly the southern states, remained deeply segregated, introducing a system of laws known as "Jim Crow" which were designed to keep the Negros in America subordinate to the whites in every way possible.

The Supreme Court of the United States ruled in May of 1954, in Brown vs. Board of Education, that public schools must be desegregated throughout the land. The verdict infuriated those whose desire was to have "two" Americas: one white and one black, one free and one in servitude, one superior and one inferior.

Dr. King, recognizing the need for reconciliation between the races and their opposing views, would use "nonviolent resistance" as his instrument of change.

Throughout his remaining years, Dr. King would stay faithful to his belief in nonviolent resistance as a means to achieve justice and equality. His character, courage, and conviction are some of the reasons why he is still revered a half century after his untimely death.

I share with you a review of one of his many sermons that I believe will assist you as you think about your career and the impact you wish to have on your company and your community.

Dr. King commented that for us to be successful we must have Tough Minds and Tender Hearts.

A Tough Mind and a Tender Heart

"Be therefore wise as serpents, and harmless as doves" (Matthew 10:16, KJV).

In this sermon, Dr. King stresses the need for us to be able to maintain balance. He uses the idea of holding two opposing thoughts in one's mind at the same time. Dr. King would state

> *"The militant are not generally known to be passive, nor the passive to be militant. Seldom are the humble self-assertive, or the self-assertive humble. But life at its best is a creative synthesis of opposites in fruitful harmony."*[1]

---

[1] Martin Luther King Jr., Strength to Love, p.1.

Dr. King would use the text found in Matthew 10:16 where he acknowledges Jesus recognizing the need for blending opposites.

Dr. King would argue that Jesus understood and knew that his disciples would face challenging times in their role of carrying out the great commission and bringing the knowledge of Jesus to the known world.

The ability to dissolve a tense situation while simultaneously recognizing the opportunity to offer salvation would be required of the disciples.

The lessons of Christ were essential and critical gifts the disciples would need to witness and extend the life of Christ to others.

Jesus would warn them by saying:

"Behold, I send you forth as sheep in the midst of wolves."

In order for them to operate successfully, Jesus would continue "be therefore wise as serpents, and harmless as doves."

Dr. King would take from this sermon the need for us to have both a tough mind and a tender heart.

The tough mind would help discern the immediacy of any dangers confronting the individual (s) or society. It would also help with the ability to make wise decisions.

However, Dr. King recognized that in our society rarely do we have an abundance of tough-minded or tough thinking individuals. He would point to the gullibility of many of us when it comes to impulse buying from TV and radio commercials and newspaper ads.

> *"This undue gullibility is also seen in the tendency of many readers to accept the printed word of the press as final truth. Few people realize that even our authentic channels of information-the press, the platform, and in many instances the pulpit, -do not give us objective and unbiased truth. Few people have the toughness of mind to judge critically and to discern the true from the false, the fact from the fiction. Our minds are constantly being invaded by legions of half-truths, prejudices, and false facts. One of the great needs of mankind is to be lifted above the morass of false propaganda."* [2]

Dr. King would speak regarding the many challenges that soft minded individuals would face, the superstitions they would hold dear and the traditions they would maintain.

> *"The soft-minded man always fears change. He feels security in the status quo, and he has an almost morbid fear of the new."* [3]

Dr. King would not limit soft mindedness to the individual. He recognized that soft mindedness had also infiltrated our institutions. Soft mindedness in religion, he observed, caused one to believe that science and religion were at odds. Dr. King believed that science and religion complemented one another.

---

[2] King Jr., ibid., p.3.

[3] King Jr., ibid., p.3.

Dr. King would say science investigates; religion interprets.

Science gives man knowledge that is power; religion gives man wisdom that is control. Science deals mainly with facts; religion deals mainly with values. The two when properly viewed, are seen as complementing versus competing.

Dr. King would also acknowledge that soft-mindedness in governments, countries, and states could lead to the rise of dictators who would capitalize on the soft mindedness of the individuals. He recognized this soft mindedness could lead to barbarity and terror in the civilized world.

> *"Adolf Hitler realized that soft mindedness was so prevalent among his followers that he said, "I use emotion for the many and reserve reason for the few."—By means of shrewd lies, unremittingly repeated, it is possible to make people believe that heaven is hell-and hell, heaven . . . The greater the lie, the more readily will it be believed."*[4]

Finally, Dr. King would assert that soft-mindedness is one of the primary causes of racial prejudice. Soft-minded people would readily believe that one race is superior over the other race. Despite all of the research that disproves that theory, segregationists believed that Negroes were lacking in academic, health, and moral standards.

> *"There is little hope for us until we become tough-minded enough to break loose from the shackles*

---

[4] King Jr., ibid., p. 4.

of prejudice, half-truths, and downright ignorance. The shape of the world today does not permit us the luxury of soft mindedness. A nation or a civilization that continues to produce soft-minded men purchases its own spiritual death on an installment plan."[5]

Dr. King would argue that while it was important for us to have tough-mindedness, we must also continue to cultivate a tender heart. He would declare it fruitless to simply focus on a tough mind yet lack the compassion of a tender heart. A tough-minded person would find it difficult to establish relationships, or see people as people, if he or she did not also have a tender heart. Such a person would often remain isolated from the joys and sorrows that others feel because of their own self-centeredness.

"The hardhearted person never truly loves. He engages in a crass utilitarianism that values other people mainly according to their usefulness to him."[6]

Dr. King would say that Jesus condemned the rich fool not because he was not tough-minded, but rather, because he was not tenderhearted.

"Jesus reminds us that the good life combines the toughness of the serpent and the tenderness of the dove. To have serpentlike qualities devoid of dovelike

---

[5] King Jr., ibid., p. 5.

[6] King Jr., ibid., p.6.

qualities is to be passionless, mean, and selfish. To have dovelike without serpentlike qualities is to be sentimental, anemic, and aimless. We must combine strongly marked antithesis."[7]

Dr. King urged his audiences to maintain the appropriate balance. He understood to move forward would require a certain toughness of mind for the Negro.

He stated that we could not simply adjust to the dictates of the segregationists and live passively as second-class citizens solely to avoid confrontation with white segregationists. On the other hand, Dr. King also understood that we couldn't drink from the cup of hatred and use weapons of violence if we desired to pass on a legacy of redemption, reconciliation, and peace to our children.

He argued that violence and hatred only begets more violence and hatred.

"Violence brings only temporary victories; violence, by creating many more social problems than it solves, never brings permanent peace. I am convinced that if we succumb to the temptation to use violence in our struggle for freedom, unborn generations will be the recipients of a long and desolate night of bitterness, and our chief legacy to them will be a never ending reign of chaos."[8]

---

[7] King Jr., ibid., p.6.

[8] King Jr., ibid., p.7.

Dr. King in this sermon would remind the listeners of the opportunity to use nonviolent resistance as a means to secure freedom. Nonviolent resistance would give them an opportunity to display their dignity, courage, and love, while dismantling the walls of racism, segregation, and poverty.

> *"We must work passionately and unrelentingly for full stature as citizens, but may it never be said, my friends, that to gain it we used the inferior methods of falsehood, malice, hate, and violence."[9]*

Dr. King would conclude this sermon by stressing a few of the attributes that belong to God. He would highlight grace and justice as two of God's attributes. In sharing these attributes, he was demonstrating to his congregation that our God was a God of balance. He spoke of God's outstretched hands and declared that one hand represented justice and tough mindedness and the other hand was representative of grace and tender heartedness.

Maintaining a life of balance is key to our growth and maturity. There will be times in our lives where we will seek either the justice of God or the grace of God depending on our circumstances and situations.

> *"When days grow dark and nights grow dreary, we can be thankful that our God combines in his nature a creative synthesis of love and justice that will lead*

---

[9] King Jr., ibid., p.8.

us through life's dark valleys and into sunlit pathways of hope and fulfillment."[10]

Every believer who embarks on the journey to succeed inside the environment of corporate America must do so with their eyes wide open. They must know that their ultimate success will not be measured in perks, privileges, and promotions, but rather in their demonstration of working as unto the Lord.

> *"Whatever you do, work at it with all your heart, as working for the Lord, not for men, since you know that you will receive an inheritance from the Lord as a reward. It is the Lord Christ you are serving" (Colossians 3:23–24, NLT).*

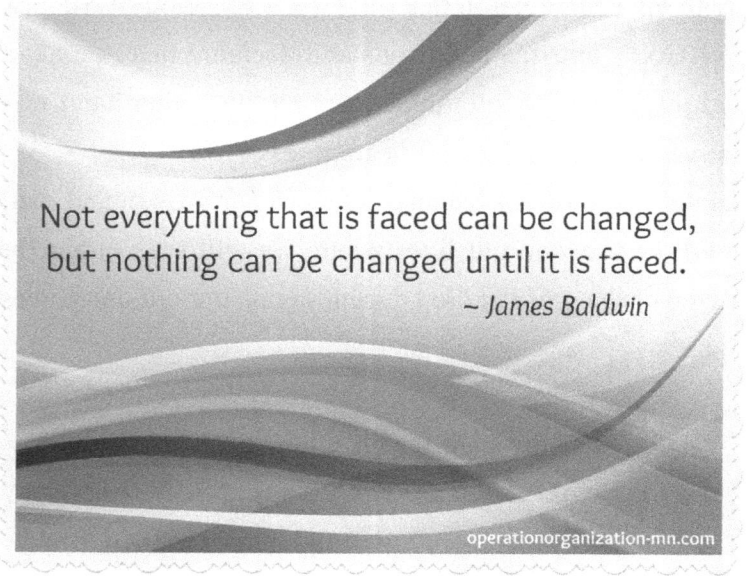

---

[10] King Jr., ibid., p.10.

Bibliography

Blanchard, K., & Hodges, P. (2005). *Lead Like Jesus : Lessons from the Greatest Leadership Role Model of All Time*. Nashville: W Publishing Group.

Boyte, H. C. (1984). *Community Is Possible: Repairing America's Roots*. New York: Harper & Row.

Covey, S. R. (1990). *Principle-Centered Leadership*. New York: Simon & Schuster.

Dungy, T., & Whitaker, N. (2010). *The Mentor Leader*. Carol Stream: Tyndale House Publishers, INC.

Hendricks, J. O. (2006). *The Politics of Jesus*. New York: Three Leaves Press.

Hillman, O. (2007). *TGIF-Today God Is First*. Ventura: Regal Books.

Ines, T. (2016). The Power Of Adding Value. *Leader To Leader*, 54–58.

Jakes, T. (2002). *Ten Commandments of Working in a Hostile Environment*. Dallas: Potter"s House.

Johnson & Johnson. (2016, May 2). Retrieved from WWW.jnj.com/Official_Site

Schein, E. H. (1999). *The Corporate Culture Survival Guide : Sense and Nonsense About Cultural Change*. San Francisco: Jossey-Bass Publishers.

Tip Poon, B. (2013). *LoopTail*. New York: Hachette Book Group.

Webster, M. (1991). *Webster's Ninth New Collegiate Dictionary*. Sprinfield: Merriam-Webster Inc.

www.ingramcontent.com/pod-product-compliance
Ingram Content Group UK Ltd.
Pitfield, Milton Keynes, MK11 3LW, UK
UKHW022223230426
12048UKWH00016BA/1030